Black Teacher

Thomas Jones

ISBN: 1-4564-3338-5
ISBN-13: 9781456433383

Prologue

When I decided to get involved in the education system, I thought surely that the system was dedicated to students. A black teacher in America can surely find success and be a positive role model to those young people with eager minds. Like most Americans, I knew that racial issues existed in the years past but believed the ground work and foundation had been laid to alleviate the stereotypical racial problems that once plagued the educational system. I thought long gone were the days when the white administration and the white teaching faculty were a part of a denigrating and condescending body that viewed other races as beneath them. Imagine my utter amazement, surprise and disappointment when I realized just how naïve I was.

I could argue that it was my lofty hopes and dreams for a more progressive America that took me down this path but I have concluded it was unbridled naiveté! I was naive enough to think that race was no longer an issue in this profession. I thought teaching had to be one profession that was committed to and capable of ensuring that all children were treated and educated fairly. Furthermore, I thought that no one involved in the educational system would allow race to play a part in disrupting that process. I guess one of my unarticulated assumptions was that the educational system attracted people committed to the equitable treatment of children. I believed that teachers were a constant example of how not to be prejudice; and leading by example was a staunch motto to which all teachers were committed. In my mind, teachers were the epitome of acceptance, regardless of race, gender, or ethnicity. After all, with education and insight, one would think, there comes a clear and self-evident understanding that intelligence does not vary amongst the races.

Unfortunately, for far more white teachers than one would think, this theory of equal intelligence is not a fundamental assumption that informs how they instruct and interact with their students. That mindset along with the same mindset that many white parents have makes it difficult for a black teacher in the school system. In the following pages, I will cite a number of situations and events that took place at different schools that illustrate how, on the surface, white America to prove that racism is not still present, when in fact it is still alive and well. I hasten to add, however, it is better camouflaged than in years past. Although I will focus on one school in particular, other scenarios will also be from different schools. Alarmingly, this pernicious racism among educators exists in more schools than we would think! The names of the schools and the names of those persons involved will not be the exact names of those schools or those persons involved. The names have been changed as to not bring those mentioned into any undue or unwelcome criticism or publicity.

Introduction

What is the state of the black teacher in this day and time since the 13th Amendment abolished slavery in the United States over 140 years ago? What battles are Black teachers fighting, other than the media's everyday portrayal of the idea that their Black race commits egregious crimes and is imploding. Black teachers are constantly dealing with their white counterpart's superiority complex. Black teachers are dealing with the lack of respect of white students whose parents have—some deliberately and some unwittingly—taught their children to have for the black teacher.

What might have transpired to have embedded such racially charged ideas and perceptions that appear to now be held by so many? I offer the following reflections as the likely attitudes that black teachers are encountering as they are teaching in many parts of this "great" country called the United States of America.

"Black teacher, are you serious? Do you really think you deserve the same common decency and respect as a white teacher in this white state? How dare you have the audacity to believe that things have changed? Do you really believe that your education places you on the same level as these white teachers whose ancestors built this country? How can you possibly believe that you have earned the right to look these distinguished white teachers in the eye and speak to them as if you are their equal?"

"Well, black teacher, you may believe that to be the case but that does not mean that you are going to be shown the same common decency and respect that is shown to your white counterparts. You may have an education but it is by no means on par with that of your white counterparts. Furthermore, you are only here because affirmative action has forced us to allow you access. You will not be given the privilege of looking me in the eye to speak to me, as I am your equal. No, I will not give you that satisfaction. I will stand strong, and as you walk past me, I will not look your way. Though you may speak I will not speak back as no one can force me to respect you as my equal."

Black teacher, do you dare contradict me when I tell you that something has not been done in the manner in which I think you should have done it? Do you dare question my authority? If you dare, I can still rely upon the "good ol' boy" network of calling upon your superiors to put in your place? It is obvious that your modern characteristic of naturally being angry and defensive is the basis for which question my decisions. What else could produce the courage in you to question my authority?

Black teacher, don't you know that I control the aspirations of your athletic youth, including those who desire to participate in sports in hopes of receiving an athletic scholarship? You may coach them but your role must be to assist me and when I make decisions on the future of your young black athletic stars yours is to back me, not to question me. Should you decide to question me you can be replaced and the administration will undoubtedly co-sign my decision. This is your creed to remember: Know your place and stay in your place.

Black teacher, don't you know that I control the collegiate and corporate aspirations of your intellectually gifted youth. Not only do I control the way "you" are incorporated in the system, I also control the way your Latino brothers and sisters may participate within the system. You may think all is well. Actually, all is well because the "good ol boy" network and our way of doing things, is alive and well indeed!

Chapter 1. Reputation Confirmed

My first job in a school setting was in a high school in Northern Virginia. Just prior to accepting the position of Achievement / Behavior Specialist, I learned that the school had an infamous reputation. Anytime I spoke to someone who grew up in the area and I mentioned that I worked at the School, they immediately offered their condolences at my having to take on such a task. They would not only reinforce the reputation for unruly behavior but also add their personal experiences. The school was located near a military base and coupled with a recent increase of military personnel whom had children and with the proximity being so close along with a recent influx of Latin immigrants, the school had a highly multi-cultural student population. The diversity of the student population—a range of languages, variance of English proficiency, economics, etc—changed the teaching environment significantly. In years past, most teachers had taught only white students and interacted only with white teachers. However, this same group of teachers was now forced to interact with people from entirely different cultures than theirs.

This infamous school was Garrison High School and was situated in an area that inadvertently encouraged delinquency of some of the students. It was located on a street that happened to have a mall just across the street from it and the students would often leave the school grounds to amuse themselves with the sights of the mall. Some, after having their fun would decide to come back to school and in so doing had to encounter the scrutiny of school security or of teachers who just so happened to have hall duty. It was common practice to have teachers patrol the schools hallways during their planning period. It was a practice that the teachers often vociferously objected to but performed the duty nonetheless. As a result, some of the teachers would become a bit more aggressive when they dealt with the students they encountered. Some of the students were cooperative, presenting a hall pass upon request. Unfortunately, there was a common issue that arose. The problem was that the pass they sometimes/often presented was a forged pass. It was a pass that that they or some other student had managed to steal from a teacher or principal. As a result, thanks to some of the conscientious security staff, many would be escorted to the principals' office to be disciplined for leaving school grounds without permission. Others would showcase their defiance by either ignoring the attending teacher and walking on, or simply becoming belligerent with the teacher for having the "audacity" to question them. As sad as it is for me to admit this, these belligerent students were often black students. I find it also relevant to mention that black students accounted for 10% of the school's student population during the subjected period.   On several occasions I observed an older white teacher continuously move in front of the students, to try to obstruct the path of those students who chose to ignore the teacher. This, of course upset the teacher just as much or more than the student. This upset the teacher because he had not come to grips with the fact that the students of this generation have a lack of respect for authority, and it upset the student because the students of this generation have a lack of respect and understanding that an adult, black or white, making a reasonable request should be obeyed. Yes_ "obey"! That is a term, should we as a society, come back to would bring about the respect that adults should be accorded when dealing with children. I know many would want to say there should be mutual respect, but when we as adults come to understand that students are not our friends deserving of mutual respect but we as adults are deserving of having children obey our reasonable request. Unfortunately, this fundamental principle also had racial overtones that presented themselves in the school.

What I have seen is the difference in attitude a white teacher takes when disrespect comes from a white student compared to the disrespect coming from a black student. After having the opportunity to observe the interactions, on several occasions, of one particular teacher with black students I finally asked him why, it seemed to me, he was sometimes fair and other times his motives in his treatment of black students seemed to be racist.

His name was Mr. Hagan. He was a white teacher who had been teaching for 20 years. He was a broad shouldered stout man in his late 40's, standing about

6'2" tall and weighed about 220 pounds. He was a clean-shaven man with graying hair seemingly from a military background in his adherence to demanding respect from others. I learned that Mr. Hagan had grown up in Virginia only a little further south than the high school in which we were in. Growing up in his southern town there were no black people and he did not encounter any himself until he was close to 15 years of age. He, however, had grown up with his father constantly instilling in him that he should never trust black people, they were no good and that he should strive to keep his race pure.

Although there were many incidents in which I could use to illustrate the way in which Mr. Hagan's prejudice stood out I will only expound upon three. Two of which he chose some common racist phrases to use toward the students and one that made me decide to talk to him about his treatment of the black students.

The first incident was his approach to dealing with a black student by the name of Danny Rogers. Danny was an intelligent young black man whose mother and father were both assistant principals in different middle schools. As an elementary and middle school student Danny was an honor roll student. He rarely received any mark lower than a "B" on any assignment in which he was a part of. In elementary and middle school he was the kind of student that most teachers would enjoy having in their classes. He was respectful and always willing to help out in the class. Although he was not the class president and made no attempt to become it, he did have the characteristics of someone who could have vied for and excelled in the role.

When Danny came into Garrison High School those characteristics disappeared when it came to academics but were apparent in his interactions with those students were less inclined to appreciate an education. He no longer put forth the effort to achieve high marks on individual assignments and was a reluctant participant on group assignments. He was often out of class for a variety of reasons, either making up a reason to have to leave class, being put out of class, or just not going to class at all. He was now disrespectful when the opportunity presented itself and had become the kind of student that most teachers hoped not to have in their class.

I have a couple of theories as to what might be the contributors or causes of those changes. One is that as Danny came into high school he was allowed more freedom than in the past. With both of his parents being assistant principals, their time was more occupied with other kids than their own. They had duties that kept them at school for longer hours and often required them to attend evening activities for their respective schools. As a result, Danny was free to spend his time as he pleased and as long as he didn't cause any emergency situations, his parents were unaware of what was going on in his life. They didn't have or did not make the time to attend after school activities that would have allowed for them to know the state of things involving Danny's academics and behavior. As a result, probably because of the lack of guidance, Danny became the rebellious student that he was. He had no one to discuss his dreams and/or problems with other than his peers who had not had enough life experiences to give him the proper advice and guidance.

Another theory is that when Danny came into Garrison High School it was at a time when he was very impressionable. At that time, what seemed to be the same time, gang activity in the school was peaking. With that and the absence of parental supervision at home it made it possible for gang members to easily lure him into their midst. They held the promise of family that he may have felt he was lacking. They would always be there for him and why wouldn't they? After all, they had no responsibilities. The idea of keeping up grades became an unnecessary desire for him. Being in a gang often required him to be rebellious to any authority other than the gang leaders and that was the attitude he adopted. That rebellion against authority is what brought him into a confrontation with the aforementioned Mr. Hagan.

Danny, after being kicked out of one of his classes for defiance was walking the halls in the school. This just so happened to be at the same time that Mr. Hagan was assigned hall duty. As I mentioned, few teachers liked the idea of having to play "hall monitor" but reluctantly performed the duty. As Mr. Hagan was patrolling his area, Danny approached. He asked Danny to see his hall pass and Danny ignored him. As he walked toward Danny, he asked again. Danny, with a scowl on his face, looked at him and continued to walk past Mr. Hagan. That open defiance vividly annoyed Mr. Hagan. In a more

Mr. Hagan walked after Danny and as he got closer to him, stated more demandingly, to Danny, "Hey boy, you hear me talking to you!"

At that moment, Danny stopped and turned to him and in a defensive tone and seemingly in an attempt to try to sound forceful stated "Who the f—k you talking to? Don't call me boy; I'm a man just like you". At that instant Mr. Hagan turned red and began walking towards him and, shouting he said, "I'm talking to you boy and you will never be a man to me, you don't know what it means to be a man. The problem with you people is that you don't appreciate how good you have things these days. When I was your age you could be lynched for talking to me like that". Needless to say Mr. Hagan had now added insult to injury in Danny's mind and Danny launched back, "Yea that was in your day, we ain't in yo' day now we in mine and I can put my foot up your ass". That seemed to be a remark that Mr. Hagan was hoping for as he was upon Danny now and said "I sure would like to see you try, don't just talk about it go ahead and do something or are you just all talk?" The challenge was now laid down, but did Danny have the fortitude or the desire to face that challenge. Danny did not say a word; he just gave Mr. Hagan a constant, and what he probably perceived as, a menacingly fierce stare. I believe he had sized Mr. Hagan up and recognized that with Mr. Hagan standing about 6'2" tall and weighing about 220 pounds and his standing about 5'6" tall and weighing only about 175 pounds this might not be the fight for him to chance. Fortunately for Danny, at that time the schools' security guard who had been en route had shown up to escort Danny to the principal's office for discipline. He immediately escorted Danny away and asked Mr. Hagan to put the incident in writing.

The second incident was with Lisa Dessier. Lisa Dessier was a mixed student (black and white) who often missed school and when she did come to school, she did not want to put forth any.. When she was in school, she had a mild disposition and was somewhat respectful when in the presence of the teachers and administration. I say somewhat respectful because, as long as no one tried to encourage her to do anything she did not want to do she was polite. However, when someone pushed her to participate academically, she usually made subtle smart remarks to let them know that she did not appreciate their efforts. She put forth little effort in completing assignments when in class and homework was not even a consideration for her. She did, as it would seem, just enough to keep the teachers from "stressing" her about completing her assignments while in class. Teachers had come to understand that, if they left her alone, they did not have to worry about her subtle remarks and it was less stressful for them in the classroom. She could be approached but once she had stated how she felt, she didn't expect the teachers to bother her any further. If the teachers did not leave her to her desires, a confrontation would take place.

The year could go on without incident if all of her teachers were that appeasing. Lisa, however, was also a student in Mr. Hagan's classroom and he was not concerned with her disposition or subtle remarks and would not accept her menial effort in his class. Such as it was, Lisa was in his class on a day when it seemed that he was fed up with a lack of student effort in general and Lisa was having one of her worst days. She had been unexpectedly confronted by two other teachers earlier and was now in Mr. Hagan's classroom. He approached her about being sure that she completes her assignment before the class was over and she, of course, took offence to it. She told him in no uncertain terms that she was working and she did not need him bothering her if she is doing her work. He, of course, took offence at her remark as a lack of respect and told her in no uncertain terms that he is the adult, the teacher in the classroom and he will not allow her to speak to him in that manner. As I mentioned, Lisa would be polite until a teacher pushes her for effort. In this situation, a confrontation was inevitable. She told Mr. Hagan that she "didn't care who he was and he better leave her alone". Mr. Hagan let her know that the classroom was his, he was not going to leave her alone and that she was not going to talk to him in that manner. He said to her, "Obviously, you have some white blood in you somewhere and you would think that some of that would come out to show that you have some manners". That statement sent Lisa into a rage and the curse words began to flow from Lisa's mouth like a waterfall in the Amazon forest. It seemed that with the same amount of pressure that the water would make at the bottom of a waterfall those words hit Mr. Hagan. Those words hit him so hard he could no longer control to his temper and he began to yell at her at the top of his lungs. "You're coming with me young lady, I am not going to stand for this, I am tired of putting up with you people and your attitudes. Somebody needs to put you in your place and if we weren't in this school I would put you in yours right now." I thought now was the time that Lisa was going to attack him with the viciousness of a savage tiger. Surprisingly, Lisa got up from her desk and followed him down to the principals' office.

Once in the office Mr. Hagan stated his case and the principal told him to write a referral for disciplinary action and he would take care of it. This also enraged Mr. Hagan and he stated, "Is that it? Just write a referral and you will take care of it. "What?" "Tell her not to do it again and then I have to see her in my classroom again after the manner in which she has spoken to me. It would be an outrage if she were allowed back in my classroom again." Not even waiting for an answer back, he left the office in an exasperated manner. After he left the office, Lisa was allowed to state her case. She told the principle her version of what happened, the things that Mr. Hagan had said to her in hopes that something would be done to him for what he had said to her. Lisa was given three days of out of school suspension, but no punishment was given to Mr. Hagan. After three days of out of school suspension, Lisa was allowed back in school and back in Mr. Hagan's classroom. The irony was there was nothing Lisa could do to him about his remarks to her, although they were egregiously offensive, and there was nothing Mr. Hagan could do about Lisa being allowed back into the classroom. He did, however, have the peace of mind of knowing that he could continue treating minority students in the manner in which he felt was appropriate. That is whether it was truly appropriate or not.

The third incident with Mr. Hagan occurred between him and Lydia Harper. Lydia was a black student who put forth good effort in school her first two years of high school but in her last two years that effort deteriorated more and more each year. She was a pleasant young girl who just seemed to struggle with the workload in her junior and senior year of high school. She was in a position of having to take two English classes and two History classes in her senior year in order to be able to graduate with the class with whom she had started. High school life, at that moment, was not quite going how she was hoping. With all of that she had the unfortunate privilege of being assigned to a Mr. Hagan's History class.

Having success in a situation requiring a student to double up on classes can be extremely difficult for a conscientious student. Of course, it is even tougher for a student who has not always performed that well. She did have the fact that the schools grading system was based on quarters in her favor. If a student passes three quarters they pass for the year. If they pass only two quarters but with a high enough quarter average, they could still pass for the year. However, if a student only passed two quarters and those quarters happened to be at the beginning of the year a teacher could use their discretion and fail the student. And it could work the other way around also. If a student failed the first two quarters but passed the last two the teacher could use their discretion and pass the student. In this, her senior year, Lydia struggled in all of her classes but managed to pass all of her classes for the first quarter. She just did get a high enough average in those double classes to earn a "D" for the first quarter in each of the classes. The second quarter was not so kind to her and she received an "F" in both of her double classes and a "D" in all her other classes. With that scenario she could not afford to fail either of her double classes for the quarter if she wanted a realistic chance to graduate with her class. If she failed either of those classes, chances were highly unlikely that she would succeed in passing the same class, in the final quarter, with a high enough grade average to allow her to pass the class for the year.

Knowing that was the situation and she had began the quarter in Mr. Hagan's class with failing marks she went from decent effort to minimal or no effort when she was in his class and was not turning in her homework. Mr. Hagan, surprisingly to me, approached her about her situation and let her know that he "was hoping that she would have put forth more effort when the quarter began and that if she had she would not be in this situation". What really surprised me was that he offered her an avenue to pull herself out of the state of desperation that she was now in. He told her that he would still accept all of the assignments that she had not turned in and if she was willing he would gladly assist her during lunch or after school if she needed extra help. Although she accepted his offer, she did not follow through with her part of the bargain and of course she failed the class and did not graduate with her class. Mr. Hagan had tried, although unsuccessfully, to help a minority student establish a goal for herself that would have given her the possibility to be successful.

With those situations in mind I approached Mr. Hagan and asked him why he had put forth the effort to help Lydia? I let him know that based on other situations I was aware with him and other students of color, including those with Danny and Lisa, I viewed him as someone who was a racist. Based on all past experiences I had witnessed with him and other students of color I did not expect him to be accepting of my approaching him. I fully expected him to become defensive and refuse to speak to me on the subject.

To my astonishment he began to open up to me about things in his personal life. He told me how he had grown up prejudiced and had held a low opinion of people of color. He described situations that he had with people of color who had reinforced the stereotypes he held. Most of his interactions with people of color had been in confrontational circumstances simply because he may have looked at someone in a way that they did not like and an argument ensued. He talked about how he had been in grocery stores with black kids in the vicinity and their pants were hanging off of them and every other word was "nigger" or "f—k this" or "f—k that". He talked about how rude and disrespectful the black students he first taught were. He talked about the lack of effort from most of the black students he initially taught.

All of those things he said made him think that his father was right about black people and that it would benefit him to keep that in mind as the school became more and more integrated. This he said was his mindset, until he had kids of his own. What he told me next was profound. He told me that it was not just his having kids but his daughter decided to marry a black man. This he said was a very, very difficult thing for him to accept. He told me that although his father had instilled in him the need to be prejudiced, he had raised his kids to view people as individuals and not use race to judge anyone. He said that initially, he had felt that he had made a mistake by raising his daughter that way because had he raised her to become prejudiced, she would have never chosen a black man to marry.

Still, he said, she had done it and it was up to him to now accept this man in his life and not look down upon him. He had to become the type of person that he had raised his daughter to be. If not, he would have to take the chance of ostracizing his daughter for living according to the principles he had taught her as being what can often establish a person as being a good or bad person. In doing so, he would turn her life upside down as she might feel that her life had been lived within a lie. He decided that was not the way he wanted to end his relationship with his daughter. He admitted that it had taken a number of years for him to feel truly comfortable around the young man when he came into his home but that, in fact, he had come to that point. He also admitted that after getting to know the young man, he learned that he was respectful, intelligent, and conscientious. He treated his daughter respectfully and she seemed to love him and was happy. After all, isn't that what all parents want for their children when they decide to get married?

As we talked he told me that those situations that I had recounted about his varying treatment of students of color were just what they seemed. He said that there were times when he reacted naturally, the way in which his father had taught him, with racist thoughts being the driving force and other times with unbiased, natural human emotion being the driving force. He told me that I have to try to understand that something that had been driven into him for 30 years could not possibly be defeated overnight. He said that it was a constant battle he deals with within himself and sometimes the racist side wins. He admitted that he may never win the battle but he will surely continue to try. He said that he also understands that most people will not know his story so they will not know the battle he is facing and some may only have an opportunity to see the racist side and label him a racist for life.

I don't believe that there is anything that he can do about that, all he can do is to continue to fight that battle and hopefully more people will see the positive side of his personality. Mr. Hagan is a rare case in his honesty about his racist views and about his daughter marrying a black man. There are many who will put on the facade that they are unbiased Americans while they routinely attend white supremacist meetings. There are many who have sons and daughters who have married people of color but they have refused to acknowledge the marriage and often will disown their own children as a result of their inability to accept that marriage.

Thomas Jones

Those who have the mindset that whites are superior are still in place. They continue to make the decisions on how this America operates. They continue to operate within our school system below the radar. With that in mind what makes you think that racism is not still in place?

It is worth mentioning that Mr. Derrick, the white principal of Garrison High School, was, in my opinion, fair and balanced in how he treated the students, regardless of race. Furthermore, he often went the "extra mile" in giving all students an opportunity to change potentially detrimental behaviors in such a manner that created an opportunity to change their individual lives. As adults, we sometimes forget they are young people learning to navigate this increasingly complex world.

Unfortunately, I have witnessed black and white teachers alike, who disagreed with his decisions, perform as a child would in displaying their discontentment. However, he maintained his composure and politely addressed any concerns that they had. I don't know that I would have been able to do the same. I also know that his efforts have not been futile. There are a few students, black and white, who, though they or their parents might not admit it, owe their having the opportunity to graduate from Garrison High School to Mr. Derrick. Although he could have had them expelled, he didn't. Instead, he gave them a chance to redeem themselves and some of them did exactly that and went on to graduate.

ֆ֍

Chapter 2. The Summit Experience

After 4 years at Garrison High School, I left to become a teacher at West Summit High School in Northern Virginia. I thought that once I left southern Virginia and went north, believing the attitudes and mindset of teachers would be more conducive than those held in the school that was in a more southern part of Virginia. I soon learned that was not the case.

The first thing I noticed was the southern dialect that has become stereotypical for the representation of white slave masters was the same in both schools. This enlightenment came in a faculty meeting. As administration and others in authority began to take the podium and address the faculty, the same southern dialect could be heard throughout the group. I noticed that the southern drawl in the way they spoke and presented themselves was very much alive and well. It might be necessary to have witnessed or have suffered from the abuses of racism to understand what I mean when I say that the atmosphere was thick with the aura of superiority that some of the white faculty members presented. There was no doubt that some of them felt that they were of a superior race.

I was faced early with having to deal with this aura of superiority with two people in power positions.

I would have thought they would have at least exhibited some basic decorum and been polite, considering their positions. Those two people were Mrs. Johnson (a teacher with whom I was sharing a room) and Mr. Hairston (West Summit's head of security). I mistakenly thought that because Mrs. Johnson knew that she had to share a room with me she might just consider that in her interactions with me. Maybe I was looking at it wrong. Perhaps she thought because she was sharing a room with me she felt it necessary to establish the understanding that she was in charge. Similarly, I thought Mr. Hairston would be more affable because his position required him to have to deal with all teachers and one would hope that he would be cordial. Suffice it to say that I was dead wrong!

I became aware of two relevant situations that had escalated to the point of having to have an assistant Principal involved. In one instance, an assistant principal had to intervene. In the other, the Principal himself was brought in to manage the matter. As a general matter, once an incident reaches a point that the administration is involved, most of the faculty who might not been involved also becomes aware of it. The circumstances of those situations will be described and the judgment is yours as to how it could or should have been dealt with.

As the school year began I was enthusiastic and looking forward to a new beginning and hopefully a new and more promising working relationship with the rest of the faculty. It became apparent to me in my first week that it might not be that easy. In that first week, upon moving into the classroom that I was sharing with Mrs. Johnson, a problem arose that immediately let me know that things might not be that easy. We not only had to share the room but we also had to share the same desk and computer. That meant that my things might be in her way at times and her things may be in my way at other times.

I was prepared to share but Mrs. Johnson was not and made me aware of her dissatisfaction with having to share with me. Toward the end of the week I came into the classroom, as the classes were changing, to prepare for my class. She happened to still be in the classroom because her class had just ended. I thought she would proceed to leave since her class was over and also to allow me to have access to the desk. That was not the case. She remained in the class and sat at the desk. As I placed my things on the desk, she gave me an angry glare that I chose to ignore. I ignored that instance and proceeded to teach the class. Later I had to ask her to excuse me to allow me to have access to the computer as we were required to enter class attendance on the computer. She begrudgingly moved out of the way for me to have access but did not move out of the chair to allow me to sit down. Once the class ended the cause of her actions were revealed. She stated that she felt that I was trying to take over the classroom and she did not appreciate it. She said that my things were all over the desk and she can't find room to put her things so that she can work. I tried to explain to her that if she would take the time to look she would see that I only used a corner of the desk and that her things cover up the rest. Her indignation really came out after that.

She made a typical statement that is made of someone who feels they are superior. She said "You people are amazing. We give ya'll an inch and you think you can take over everything." There were many thoughts running through my mind, one of which was to revert back to my days of a foolish youngster and curse her out. However, I decided that the best thing to do was to leave the room and go to the department chair and allow her to deal with the situation. I went to the department chair and explained the situation to her and let her know that before I went back into that classroom with her in there someone is going to have to help her to understand what it means to share a room. I am not sure what she said to her but for the rest of the year I had no problem with her. She would leave the room when her class period was over and I did the same. I did not say anything to her and she did not say anything to me. But I took that as one lesson learned about the attitude that white teachers in this school have about black teachers though some may not openly express it.

The incident with Mr. Hairston occurred in a few situations but they were very subtle and I wanted to be certain in my observations. If I said anything to him, my assertions would have to be solid. When someone is treated in a disrespectful way they may initially view it as coincidental. But they begin to become aware of it when things happen more than once with the same person who is disrespecting them. That's how it was with Mr. Hairston. On several occasions I had passed

Mr. Hairston in the hallway and spoke and he had either looked me right in the eye and not spoken back or just continued to walk past me as if I wasn't even there. The first two times I just thought that maybe his mind was somewhere else and he did not hear me. But when it happened on several other occasions and there happened to be a white faculty member whom I noticed he spoke to as he passed by them I felt that truly he did not speak to me because I was black and he did not feel that he needed to acknowledge me.

There was a particularly poignant example that reinforced what I felt was a lack of respect for the black faculty. On more than one occasion, Mr. Hairston would interrupt my conversation without even acknowledging that I was having a conversation with that person. I would have to say that Mr. Hairston is not the only white member of the faculty that would look me right in the eye and not speak even though I had spoken to them. There were a number of other white faculty members who would do the same.

One of those of note was Mr. Handley, who is a teacher in the History department and the head football coach. I had often spoken to him and he had never had the courtesy to return the gesture. I finally stopped trying to speak to him after a day when I spoke as he walked into the copier room and he continued to ignore me. The breaking point for me occurred because I was the only person present and I am certain he heard me. When I spoke, he simply looked at me in a dumbfounded manner and did not say a word. His true feelings about black people in general later came out in an incident with him and a black football player. The details of that incident will be recounted in chapter 4.

Mr. Handley's demeanor and attitude toward other black staff members resounded throughout the History department. There was no question of where they stood on racial issues. Other races were inferior to hiss and be aware that he was a historian and the history of white dominance was to remain secure. However, they weren't the only department with such skeletons, but theirs were more out in the open. The English department had its secrets as well. In any organization, many secrets are often revealed in an unintended ways.

Such was the case with Mrs. Parker, the white English department chair. She was a proper speaking woman who grew up in the most southern part of Virginia. She was well aware of the role the Jim Crow laws played in allowing white people to dominate black people. She expected that all black people should remain in that state of mind when it came to their interactions with her. She was not one to come right out and say it, therefore, she was just as "clever" as those who secretly tried to keep those laws in place. She demonstrated this view with actions, not words.

Mrs. Parker's true character was exposed when a black teacher, Mrs. Blake, had the audacity to question a decision by Mrs. Parker; a decision which was procedurally open for discussion during a department meeting. In the meeting Mrs. Blake and Mr. Henry were the only black teachers in attendance with Mrs. Parker and six other white teachers. The discussion centered on an issue that was really not Mrs. Parker's concern but she made it so. Mrs. Blake was in charge of deciding upon and scheduling extracurricular activities that were to be arranged for seniors to participate in. Mrs. Parker had become aware that Mrs. Blake decided not to arrange for the seniors to participate in an activity called laser tag. Although it was not really her concern, Mrs. Parker decided to open the issue up for discussion. She said that because there were teachers in the meeting who had seniors in their classes, there should be a discussion about the issue. She said that this decision should not be made by only one person, although she had never asked Mrs. Blake if the decision was made by only one person. She began by discussing the concerns that some of her senior students had brought to her. They had told her that Mrs. Blake did not give them a chance to vote on the activities that they wanted to participate in, that they have tried to discuss the issue with her but she would not discuss it with them and that their parents have tried to communicate with Mrs. Blake concerning this issue, but she was non-responsive to their telephone calls or emails. She went on to say that she would like to recommend that the activity be arranged and scheduled because these activities were for the students and not for the teachers. Furthermore, she wanted to know if any of the other teachers felt the same.

At that point Mrs. Blake spoke up and said that she understands that Mrs. Parker has her opinion of what should happen but really this is not a discussion for a department meeting. With that statement, Mrs. Parker seemed to have taken offence. With a stare and in a condescending tone, she told Mrs. Blake that it was not her place to tell her what is appropriate or inappropriate to discuss in a meeting. She went on to inform her that she was fortunate to even be able to attend a meeting that the department was having. At that point it would have been understandable if Mrs. Blake would have lost her temper and lashed back at her, but she did not. She simply stood up and walked out of the meeting, calmly opening and closing the door as she left. With the arrogance that can be expected of someone who believes they are superior to others, Mrs. Parker continued with the discussion in hopes of obtaining a consensus to reinstate the laser tag activity.

Of course that wasn't the end of it, but how it ended came as a surprise to Mrs. Blake. Believing she need not concern herself any further with Mrs. Parker and the issue, she went on about her daily activities. After all, Mrs. Parker truly had no part in the decision making process at all. At least that was what Mrs. Blake thought.

Completely caught by surprise, because she was teaching class, she was called to the office of the administrator of her department for a meeting. His name was Mr. Jenkins and he too was white. Mr. Jenkins was an obviously timid man, but was confident in his dealing with black people because he was white. Going to the meeting, Mrs. Blake thought she was going to discuss her upcoming teacher evaluation but instead it became obvious that Mrs. Parker had spoken to Mr. Jenkins about what had occurred in the department meeting.

He began by asking her how things were going in her classes and tried to seem genuinely interested. As they talked, out of nowhere, he told her that she seemed to be angry about something and asked her if there was anything that she wanted to talk about. At that point she knew that he had really called her in to discuss what had happened in the department meeting. Without letting him know that she knew where he was going with the conversation, she calmly asked him what made him think that she was angry. Still being deceptive, he said that he sensed that she was upset and just thought he would ask. She told him that she could not understand why he would sense something like that since nothing has happened during the current meeting that would suggest that she was angry.

Eventually he asked her how things were going with the senior activities. She said that things were going fine and that he could have addressed this from the beginning rather than taking the approach he had taken. Finally, he told her that he was aware that she had walked out of the department meeting and that maybe she wanted to talk about it. To be sure that he understood her version of the situation, she told him what had happened in the department meeting and that she stands by her decision. But, she said, just to clarify things and move on she would further explain her stance. She told him that it was not an issue of her not wanting to allow the students to participate in an activity that they wanted, but it was a safety issue. She had looked into the activity and was told by the school board that the activity could not be sanctioned by the school system and any negative repercussions would fall solely on her. She told him that she had given that response to the parents in an email and had the emails on hand to prove the fact. She also told him that she thought it was first inappropriate for Mrs. Harper to get involved in something that was not her concern and a complete lack of respect for her to demean her in a meeting simply because she chose to disagree with her. Secondly, she said that it was equally inappropriate for him to call her out of class to come to his office to discuss such an issue. That it should have ended with his telling Mrs. Harper that it was not her concern and that she should make sure that department meeting topics are department specific. With that, she asked if she could get back to teaching her class where she belongs.

That situation mirrors the slave mentality of the mistress calling upon her husband to "tame" a slave whom she felt was too inept to understand their place. Mrs. Harper did not just happen to come into this understanding it is something that she has undoubtedly witnessed from the time since she was a child and, it seems, hopes to continue as she grows old. Mrs. Blake was able to victoriously respond in a dignified and intellectual manner that let Mr. Jenkins and Mrs. Parker know that she will not be taken as a second class citizen. Although it is a victory for righteousness, it is a battle being fought in a war that might never be won when it comes to changing the mentality of those who have known that type of power all of their lives.

≈≈

Chapter 3. The Trickledown Effect

Before becoming a parent or having taught school, I had my own ideas of how the school system was operating. I thought teachers had it easy and that their problems were minimal. Sure, I thought that they had to occasionally deal with a class disruption but overall there weren't any real problems that teachers had to deal with. Now, after teaching for the past ten years, I have a different perspective. However, this perspective did not come after ten years of teaching it came the first time I took on a long term substitute position in the school system. During that time I found that teachers often have to be a father or mother to some of the students since many of them come from single family homes and they seem to be searching for that other parent to communicate with and may find solace in communicating with a teacher. Teachers are often a friend to some of the students as many of the students are very shy and find comfort in having the opportunity to talk to someone who would listen to them outside of their home. Teachers are also unpaid tutors for struggling students. Additionally, to say the least, they are defenders of those who often find it difficult to stand up against peer pressure.

As a black teacher, one not only has to deal with those issues with students but they also have to deal with the lack of respect from many of their white peers and some of the white students. Those white students whose parents have enforced the idea that black people are inferior to them. Those white students who were astute in their awareness of the lack of respect that their white teachers have shown to the black teachers.

As black teachers navigate trying to adapt to their white peers' perception, black teachers still have to learn their place and understand who is in control. This is an environment that can really try their patience. On one occasion, I witnessed the treatment of a black substitute teacher having to deal with a condescending white teacher. On another occasion, I witnessed the condescending tone and attitude that a white student used in communicating with a black assistant principal.

When a substitute is in for a regular teacher they have to depend upon other staff members to give them access to that teacher's classroom and often to assist in them with necessary materials. On this day a black substitute teacher needing access to the classroom asked a white teacher passing by to open the classroom door so that he could get in. The white teacher refused to open the door stating that she could not allow him to have access to another teacher's classroom. He explained to her that he was substituting for the teacher in question and had no key to get in. Satisfied with his explanation she opened the door and let him into the classroom. This would be of no real consequence had there not been two other circumstances that occurred that involved the same situation.

I had been a witness to this same teacher open the classroom door for a white substitute teacher without question. Second, the black substitute teacher was wearing a badge with SUBSTITUTE TEACHER written clearly and in bold print on it. Still, this teacher felt the need to make the black teacher take an extra step before she would acknowledge who he was. All the students who are at the door when this takes place notice how the white teacher treats the substitute. These students take their cues from the teacher as to how they should deal with the substitute and black staff members in general.

On another occasion I witnessed a black teacher practically explode while trying to maintain her composure as a white teacher spoke to her in a condescending tone. It was against the school's policy for "**students**" to use cell phones during the school day and it was expected that teachers would enforce this rule. However, not only did many teachers fail to enforce this rule but often the administrators would fail to enforce the rule also. As a result it made it difficult for the teacher who chose to enforce the rule. On this occasion, a black female teacher was making a phone call on her cell phone when a white male teacher approached her and asked her to put her cell phone away. The black teacher was, of course, offended that another teacher would have the nerve to tell her to put her phone away. Her initial thought seemed to be to put him in his place but instead she tried to handle the situation with dignity. She realized that she is young and could be mistaken for a student and did not want to make a scene. She asked the person whom she was talking with to hold on and politely let the white teacher know that she was not a student, but a teacher in hopes that he would then just leave her alone. That did not happen. He seemed to take offence to her not adhering to what he had commanded her to do. He told her that he did not care who she was and that she needed to get off of the telephone. With that being said he just turned and walked away. At that moment she was visibly upset with the situation and said goodbye to the person she was talking to on the phone and then began to walk after him. Fortunately, another black female teacher was there as the scene was unfolding and stepped in front of her preventing her from catching up with him. It is difficult to say whether it would have been better for her to have confronted him or to have left the situation as it was and address it later if it ever happened to her again. There is the dilemma that a black teacher will face, when or what occasions should be addressed and which ones are better left alone.

I have had a similar situation happen to me but not with a direct command. As I was talking on my cell phone, a white female administrator approached me and waited until I got off the phone. Once I did, she asked me to not use the phone in an area where the students can see it because it sets a bad example for the students. I asked her how it sets a bad example. She said that since the students are not allowed to use their cell phones, we should not use ours in their presence. I politely said to her that I think it is a better example for students to understand that there are things that adults can do that students cannot.

One, because I am an adult and two because I have earned that privilege and as long as I am not using it during the time I am teaching class, that should not be a problem. I further explained to her that our failing to understand that is one reason more and more students believe they should be allowed the same privileges that we have. Furthermore the more we continue to give in to how they think things should be done, the closer we get to "having the inmates running the asylum" than we are already. One thing people fail to or refuse to realize is that students haven't changed but the adult's way of dealing with them has and that is where the problem lies. As a teacher, I haven't seen a student yet who has tried anything, and I do mean anything that I didn't see students trying when I was a student and I have been out of school for 27 years. If the adults who are making the decisions don't realize that, we will continue down this terrible road of declining student motivation and discipline.

The arrogance with which some students have come to present is an amazing thing to perceive. Athletes are known for their arrogance but the all out display of it usually takes place once they have become professionals or high profile college athletes. In the case of the Lacrosse players, at West Summit High School, that display unfolds once they become part of the team. The majority of high school Lacrosse players are children of affluent parents. As stereotypical as this may sound it is none the less the truth. It requires a great deal of money to be able to participate in the sport and that fact negates that possibility of some students being able to participate. Affluence can breed confidence and along with that arrogance can sprout. It is a very difficult thing for an adult to separate the two and even more difficult for a teenager to do so. Such was the case with the lacrosse player whom Mr. Wright, the black assistant principal, encountered at West Summit High School.

Mr. Wright approached a well-known lacrosse player named Zach Prada asking him to put away his cell phone. Since cell phones are not to be used during the school day unless it is an emergency, Mr. Wright was well within his right to make the request. Defiantly, Zach responded with a quick quip, "sure Gumby" but continued to talk on the phone. Mr. Wright asked him again and reminded Zach that his name was Mr. Wright not Gumby and that he expected him to refer to him as Mr. Wright. Zach did stop talking on the phone but degradingly responded with, "whatever you say Gumby".

Incensed with the complete lack of respect, Mr. Wright asked Zach to come with him to the office because he was showing a complete lack of respect. Laughing as he walked down the hall with Mr. Wright, Zach motioned to get his friend's attention and asked "What do you think he is going to do?" Without waiting for their answer he answered, "Nothing, I haven't done anything wrong?" In his mind, he did not think he had done anything wrong. He had come to know that the adults in his life have a lack of respect for the black man.

Therefore, his lack of respect should not result in any negative consequences.

This is a state of mind that these young white males will carry with them as they graduate from high school, go on to college and eventually run the businesses that their fathers and grandfathers have run; just as they run the country. They will not have any desire to have themselves viewed as equal to other races; theirs will be to continue as their fathers have, keeping those in place whom they feel need to be kept in place. With that in mind, what will happen when they are in positions to make the decisions when it comes to their hiring process? They will have already forged relationships that will ensure that they hire people of their own "crest". While many of their peers of a different color will languish for many years trying to achieve a fraction of what they will have achieved in a short time span. One might argue that they have worked hard for that success. That might be true, but that success is easier to achieve when it has been laid out for you and the obstacles are moved to ensure that as long as you take "steps" toward your business goals, your financial goals, your personal goals will be achieved.

Their peers of a different color will have to trudge as best they can. Their task will be of breaking ground that has not existed for them. There will be no ready-made plan for them; they will have to take the time to plan for themselves, if they grasp the importance of doing so at an age that will allow for them to be successful. As they trudge forward time passes and if their plans don't go as planned, they have to revise them and hope that their new plans will be more fruitful, at the same time they are always losing ground to their white peers. This, as their white peers continue on their undaunted journey.

Contrary to their white peers, as obstacles come up for them, they have no one there to remove those obstacles. They have to figure out a way around them. This undoubtedly causes them to lose time in the race for success and that general desire to have their own business. The question becomes a simple but difficult one for them. Should they continue to strive to own their own businesses or should they give up the dream and go to work for their white counterparts? After so much time has passed they have come to an age that if they have not already started a family, they would like to. If so, they would then be looking for financial stability and that would most likely be found in their giving up their dream and going on to work for someone else. If they choose to continue to chase their dream, they risk financial hardship at a time when they are trying to provide for their families.

ॐ∙ॐ

Chapter 4. The Sporting Impact

It is a well-known stereotype, if not a completely true thought, that most blacks are well-skilled in athletics. They are the majority participating in the major American sports such as football and basketball. Still, those who have the most impact on the progression that the black athlete makes, continues to be a white person who is in charge. Such is the case in most schools in this state of Virginia.

It begins at the top in the individual schools, where 90% of the schools' principals are white. Yes, a number of minority individuals may be interviewed, but when the decision is made, the result is more of the same. That is, another white principal is hired. The "good ol' boy" network is still alive and well. Those principals are the ones who have the ultimate decision on who is hired as the athletic director, of which 99% are surely white. Sure they will go through the motions of interviewing so called "potential" candidates but they know they already know who they are going to hire. The "good ol' boy" network is still going strong. In turn, the athletic director is in charge of hiring all the coaches for the school's teams.

As a result, 90% of all the head coaches are white. Sure, they compile their list of candidates and portray to the public that they are actively seeking the best candidates, regardless of race, but the decision has already been made. The "good ol' boy" network is deeply rooted for years to come. Those head coaches aren't completely ignorant. They do understand the importance of having a black influence on their coaching staff. Hence, they will hire at least one black assistant coach. After all, they need someone who can communicate with the black athletes when they get too head-strong for them to handle. If they had their way, they would simply get rid of the player, but they are typically too proficient of an athlete for them to cut them from the team. Therefore, they delegate the task of dealing with the kid to the black assistant.

Due to the "good ol' boy" network, it becomes very difficult for a black coach to get the head coaching position. West Summit High School so happened to be one of the schools that was an exception to the rule. West Summit High School hired a black head coach. I am sure, without my telling you what sport it is, you have already guessed what that sport is. That sport is basketball. On two occasions, the administration had the opportunity to hire a black head coach for the football team, but on both occasions decided to hire a white coach who did not work in the school. Typically schools inquire within their respective school first when hiring a coach but still they chose to not hire from within. The hiring of the white coach left the black coach—who had the qualifications to be the head coach, and had been working with the team for the past five years—with a decision to make. He had to decide whether to continue as an assistant or walk away from doing something that he loved. When someone makes a decision like that they have to ask themselves how humble they can be in the situation. After all, he was as qualified as the white coach. He chose to stay because he felt that he could have more of a positive impact with the kids if he stayed.

It so happened that the power and influence that white people feel and think they have would prove that this country has not changed much. They still take advantage of this as they do things that impact the lives of people who will not bend to their will. A young, black and up and coming football player made his way into West Summit High School. He was the type of kid who did everything that he was supposed to as a player, student, and person. He conducted himself in the way that you would hope all student athletes would. However, while in the stands watching his son play, the father made a comment about some things about which he disagreed. Someone sitting in the audience heard the comment and shared them with the assistant coach. Eventually his comment made its way back to the head coach. The aforementioned History teacher in Chapter 2, Mr. Handley, via third party and the coach took offense to this black man questioning him. In an email to another coach Mr. Handley spelled out his feelings about the father and son.

Quite shockingly, [Mr. Handley/Coach] began crafting an email concerning the matter at 3:30am! The e-mail laid out his feelings about the father and his plans to put him in his place. He described how he felt that the parent was just a joke like so many of the players' parents. He described how he planned to now ruin the kid and ensure that he will not play football in any school in the county. He laid out his plan to ensure that he will put the kid through mental strains and crush his desire for football if the kid remained at the school and played football. He went on to talk about the power he has a football coach because he has built up some reputation with college recruiters and how he will destroy the kids chances of getting a scholarship and he emphasized DESTROY his chances! This is the continuation of the "good ol' boy" network because, as it is well known, the college head coaching ranks are dominated by white men.

One would think that with such an email in hand, and appointment with the principal to discuss the matter, the coach would not have remained the coach for long. To think that would only be a thought. No action was taken against him. He maintained his position as the coach. It's amazing that with that type of rhetoric he would remain in his position, having the opportunity to ruin any other kids' dreams as he so chooses. It is remarkable to think, that in 2008, someone with those views would be allowed to stay in power. But the reality is, although it is sometimes cleverly veiled, oppression continues. It is allowed to thrive even when it is 100% exposed and admittedly expressed to those who have the opportunity to halt it. Why? Because the idea that whites are superior is thriving and the "good ol' boy" network continues to pacify those who flaunt it.

In each of those cases something very interesting occurred that again brought out the reality of how those white educators who were in charge viewed their black peers. As mentioned, West Summit had taken the opportunity to hire a black teacher as the head basketball coach. When someone becomes the head coach, they view it as their program and they will construct the program in a way that fits their style and approach to coaching. Mr. Marlin, the coach whom they had hired would come to find out that although he was hired as the coach, the decisions he wanted to make would be far from being totally his own. He was often "encouraged" to make decisions that the athletic director deemed best for the program. When the coach voiced his opinions, the athletic director would reiterate his thoughts and directed the coach to adopt the decisions that he had offered as the athletic director. The coach however, had the courage to make some decisions that were contrary to what the athletic director wanted; doing what he felt was best for the program. Needless to say, he only had the pleasure of coaching the team for three years as he became what is probably the first high school coach in the state of Virginia to be fired for reasons other than conduct deemed detrimental to the school or a student. Once again it is the white man's world: Stay in your place and do as the white man says or suffer the consequences.

෨ ෨

Chapter 5. Up for Debate

I have thus far depicted events from my personal experience, on of either being made aware of the event or having witnessed it firsthand. The following is an account of a young black male teacher who narrates his account of the trials and tribulations he had to face. I became a debate coach because I needed a job. The position I originally applied for was a high school English teacher in Fairfax County Virginia. I had previously taught for a year in Atlanta, and three years in Upper Marlboro, MD. Maryland would not extend my contract one month to take a teacher certification test required for all teachers who were on track to be certified. I had heard and read that Fairfax County had better pay and better students, so I traveled across the bridge for a few interviews.

I sat down with the principal, vice-principal, and English department chair for an interview a few weeks before school started. It was one of those interviews you walk away from with confidence. I had the job! During the interview, the vice principal said I reminded him of his son, and they were all excited that I was a former drama director ready to take on the role of debate and forensics coach. The debate team was floundering. The school had a debate team, but recently a great coach had left, and a few coaches had tried and failed. Debate was a sport not embraced by everyone, especially the public school system.

I spent the first year learning what debate was and how the debate community interacted. I was the only coach in charge of two sports. Debate is an academic sport, recognized by the Virginia High School League, and Forensics is another. I managed to learn from a couple of local coaches, and filled out forms for Membership to the National Forensics League, and the Virginia Forensics League. Everything was pretty much handed to me in a package, wrapped in another package with a hundred more packages wrapped inside each other.

I had a class of about 25 students and the administration put debate and forensics together in one group with one teacher—me. The class was a dumping ground for students who had no idea what forensics was. There were students who thought forensics class was a prerequisite for some sort of FBI or CSI class. I had some of the kids who had failed Art or another elective and since there were not quite 30 kids, more were added to the mix. One administrator told me, off the record of course, that I was sort of like a test dummy, and that I was put in one of the hardest coaching positions so I would fall on my face. I decided to prove everyone wrong.

I learned how to debate and how to run a class in the first year. My students were learning how to debate by being tossed in Junior Varsity rounds, some Varsity rounds, and during class debating with me. There were tears when students lost, and we were all excited when we won a round. During awards ceremonies, we heard all the other schools being called for awards, but I knew one day I would hear my high school's name called. The administration never knew what to do to help, or if they did know, I was not a concern. I heard rumors of schools with a certain student population who were given stipends for operating a team. Apparently, debate is one of the most expensive sports to run if success is a goal. There are meets all over the country that usually start on Friday and end on Sunday afternoon. Virginia is by far one of the most competitive debate states, but I didn't know that, nor did I care. I grew to love the craft, and teaching it became a passion.

In my second year, I had decided to split debate and forensics students and teach two sports at the same time during the school day and hold practice twice a week. Students were not used to the challenge, but those who met the challenge excelled and a couple students that year made it to regional debate. The team still watched the dynasty of a nearby high school dominate the award ceremonies. I was determined to figure out how and why the other teams were so talented. Our schools had the same demographic makeup, and we offered challenging courses. There was no reason why my team should not accomplish as much or more.

I was told during my first and second year over and over again to contact the old coach. He was touted as a great coach; someone to ask for advice. I eventually looked him up and didn't find his name in any of the National Forensics League's databases, which told a different story from the one that they were telling as they touted his greatness. How could such a phenomenal coach have no credentials? When I walked around the VHSL coaches meetings, I felt like an alien. No one talked to me and I believe me, no one took me seriously enough to be a coach. I had made a couple of friends, and they are still close to me to this day. Even through all the dramatic and traumatic events that I was involved in as the Debate coach.

During my third year, I had responded to a random email from a community mom offering to help with my team. After calling back, the mom decided to join me; she refused pay, even when I tried to pay her half of my "generous" $4,000 stipend. Since I was coaching two teams, I got paid as two coaches. I would have traded $2,000 to split up the hours driving to meets, practicing after school, and teaching both sports during the school day. My assistant coach in training was very helpful, and I could not have asked for a nicer lady to go on the journey with me. My team had become a small force to be reckoned within Virginia and we started to hear our name called at award ceremonies. I even started to host tournaments with the President of the league, who showed me the ropes in the tabulation (tab) room. My team started to win, and that's when I felt the heat from the white hot sunlight of my coworkers.

Day by day, I heard less about contacting the old coach, whom I had attempted to contact but got nowhere on that quest. My coworkers knew I started to do well as the coach, and the team started to resemble a real debate team. I had students in many different forensics events, and a couple of the popular debate events, and we started to bring home trophies. We even won a district championship in 2008. The banner was not hung, and the traditional district championship picture was not even scheduled. The plaque was bare, and the numbers that were supposed to be hung in the gym were "ordered". I still have not seen the numbers for 2008, 2009, or 2010's district debate championship.

This year, after four years of learning and success, I had the number one debate team in Virginia. I checked the National Forensics League ranking every month or two, because I battled neck and neck with another dynasty that had four coaches. My assistant mom coach had moved to Richmond two years ago, and I had been on my own with a team of well over 50 students. One meeting my president had counted 75 students. I had been promoted in the league to President of Debate in Northern Virginia. I had won debate coach of the year in 2008, and my team had won so many titles in Virginia that the debate section of the trophy case was full. I asked my athletic director about the numbers in the gym and he said he would "get on that". I felt the discrimination of being a black coach little by little, and it became more and more evident that I was not everyone's favorite coach like that last great wonder who had moved to the West coast. I never imagined that in four years I would attain any of the accolades my team achieved, and I never tooted my own horn about it either. But I knew that if I were a white coach, my administrators would toot my horn. I watched other teachers receive praise for feats less impressive, although I mean no disrespect to them.

One year the team had traveled to Pennsylvania and a few Virginia High School invitational tournaments, which cost more than our usual Virginia Forensics league tournaments. We had to raise money by begging the community door to door; the band called it tag day. I didn't want to have to sell ice pops in front of the school for weeks like I had done the previous year to raise the money to pay back our account. I remember how hot it was and how the students tried to bargain with me. I walked around with a bag of ice pops for the last three weeks of school, until the principal told me that she would pay off the balance of about $240.00 with administration funds. I guess she had seen my dedication first hand. I needed help, but I couldn't convince my team to humiliate themselves. I didn't know many other ways to raise money, but I still remember thinking, "Why don't other coaches go through this?" I knew there was a fund for debate teams, but I just couldn't get the information proven as a fact. I guess I should have just asked about the fund.

With the changing of the leadership in the school, the following year had become my worst year as a teacher and debate coach. Oddly it was my most successful year if one were to look at the record books, and I'm sure my English students would attest to an amazing and challenging year full of rigorous reading and writing instruction. The new principal seemed at first to welcome me with open arms, saying he would support me in all my endeavors. He used to say, "I really enjoy your enthusiasm!" I started to hate that line, because it sort of sounded like all I had was energy and charisma, but no skill or brains. It was like an echo of what people said about Obama, the great orator. The year dragged on in the English department, with a polarization of co-workers like one of those colored oil souvenirs. The black teachers were dots floating through a maze that coagulated at the top, and met, then flipped over to go through the maze again. I got into arguments with some of the white teachers for the most trivial reasons, all of which I won't get into. The point is, success seemed like a double-edged sword, and I was standing on the tip.

My team won first place in debate again in the Virginia State Championship for the Virginia Forensics League, and we qualified for the National Championship. This is when all hell broke loose.

Prior to that success, on the way to a competition, one of my best students was feeling sick on the way to the meet. We were already running a little late due to traffic and waiting for a teammate to meet at the rock (a very large rock that sits on the lawn) in front of the school. I had to make a decision between difficult choices: one was leaving him behind, and the other was stopping to get him some Midol from CVS and a sandwich from Subway. This coach's call made us later than normal, but not late enough for disqualification. Everything was going well until one of my students was called into a meeting with me and some other coaches to discuss a possible penalty that would cause disqualification. Apparently, a coach from a rival high school had judged him during a previous meet in a different league and again in the district competition. She (WHO IS 'SHE'?) noticed a change in his piece and challenged his authenticity. Eventually our school received written violations for lateness, last minute drop of a competitor, and a disqualification of another competitor. We still won the district championship.

About a week later, three of the members of the school's leadership; my principal, vice-principal, and athletic director supposedly had a meeting and together they decided that my team would not travel to any more debate competitions, including the National Championship we had qualified for weeks beforehand. I say supposedly because I found out later that no meeting ever took place. My athletic director came into my room with his new helper, and questioned my motives before the district championship in reference to our sportsmanship violation. The meeting lasted about thirty minutes and some of the highlights were them telling me that I made the school look bad, that I was not managing the team effectively, and that I would need to plan better next year. They argued that I was not doing a good job with the team. I had to stop them there by sticking up for myself, announcing that I had brought the school another district championship. My athletic director remarked, "Oh, I didn't know that!"

Later, I went to the principal and vice principal separately about the so-called meeting they had when they had determined that I would not be able to compete in any more post-season competitions other than Virginia High School League competitions. Eventually I managed to argue that since my team had qualified for the National Championship, we had to go. It seemed like a battle I should not have had to fight, since this was the highest point of my debate career, and some of the best debate bragging rights for a principal in Virginia. This happened a few weeks before most coaches had booked rooms, and figured out who was going to the competition in June. By the time I had managed to make my case for debating in the national competition, plane tickets were very expensive, and I had to purchase my own tickets, rooms, and everything else. The challenge was not raising the money, which we attempted to do, or getting my debaters prepared for the meet. The challenge was convincing my principal that I should be allowed to accompany my team to the National Championship.

I had been reminding my principal every day to meet with me about signing official documents that allowed me to go to the competition, when one day in a staff meeting I cornered him and really pressed the issue. He said he could not imagine a coach being away from his class for a week. He added that I would have to prepare for a week off, away from my English classes. I said that the National Championship was the highlight of any coach's career. I added that the National Forensics League was almost a hundred years old and coaches have been traveling to national competitions for a week for at least 50 of them. I couldn't believe his irrational answers. It had to be because I was a young, black, successful coach. I was convinced, and everyone who I had talked to was convinced that he was off target on this one. Any other coach from any other sport that had a national competition would be allowed to go with his team. In addition, if the high school track, football, or baseball team made it to a national championship the news media would be at the school and the red carpet would be rolled out! After trying to convince my principal at that staff meeting, he said he would think about it and he passed me a bottle of water. I left.

The next time I saw him he said he would call the principal at a nearby high school to discuss the situation. I am a close friend of the coach there, and she was allowed to go to the championship before. Needless to say, he never called that principal. I scheduled another meeting with him and after meeting in his office with a few key members of the debate team. He finally made the decision to allow me to go. One member of my debate team had qualified after trying for three years, two of them were new to the team, and one had managed to qualify despite battling cancer while going through surgery and chemotherapy. We waited outside of his office while he was chitchatting to with vice-principal, who was his buddy from years ago, before he allowed us to come in to see him. One of the debaters broke into tears outside the office because she was so stressed about the situation and because of the pressure created by the principal and her teachers. As a result, she pulled out at the last minute and would not go into the meeting. Luckily, another debater volunteered to go in. In the office we argued for about 45 minutes stating several different reasons why I should be able to go with my team, and how important it was for the school. The principal said that football was more important because it was a big money maker for the school, and if the football team made it to something like this it would be great. He also said that he would be against the decision if he allowed it. Finally, after I pushed the paperwork in front of him, he said plainly, "Don't plan on doing this again next year." I was dumbfounded. At that point I quit in my head, but I still made it to Kansas City to carry on with the competition. There was no help from the administration in getting ready, no announcement of the team going, and no more pats on the back in the hallway or statements of great enthusiasm.

While I was at the debate tournament, the coach from the school my principal was supposed to call told me there was a funding account that each debate team in Fairfax County was able to use. The account was for yearbook, journalism, and debate. The amount of money in the fund was *more* than enough to support debate, which was described as an important activity, but expensive to run and difficult to raise funds for. I asked my athletic director, principal, and the finance officer about it and they denied the existence of the fund. My principal actually said, "I doubt that." The finance officer eventually admitted that she knew about the fund, but said that I would have had to use the account number on the request for funding. That was great advice, but how was I supposed to use a funding account number for something I had no idea existed? The journalism teacher and the yearbook advisor used the account, and it should have been offered to me from the first date of hire. I believe my five-year dedication as a debate coach would have been even more successful if I didn't have to sell ice pops, or worry about each paid judge, or registration fee.

At the same time I was dealing with the debate issues, I was going through a battle with the English department, which was the department that same vice-principal oversaw. Apparently the students of my freshman pre-AP Honors English class told him that they felt that they were not being prepared for tenth grade honors English. When the vice principal and the department chair had shared this information, I was floored. I immediately told them to check my students' writing journals, which had writing prompts similar to AP tests, SAT's and advanced writing classes. I told them to go over every lesson that I had planned for the entire year. I stated that the first book they read and annotated was Ernest Hemmingway's *The Old Man and the Sea*. The books and plays read up to that day consisted of *Romeo & Juliet, The Odyssey, The Narrative of the Life of Frederick Douglas, Night,* works by *Edgar Allen Poe,* and more short stories that were especially challenging. I used multi-genre research project ideas from my Northern Virginia Writing project class at George Mason University. I taught my students over 75 literary elements, and they were familiar with Socratic Seminars and peer editing writing groups. The list goes on and on, but my point is that no student or few students can assess their teacher's ability to prepare them for the following grade. They cannot, as they have not been in such a class to know the content. Still, the department chair decided that because of my "inability" to teach pre-AP/Honors 9, I would be moved to 12th grade English. She literally stated that she didn't think I was equipped to teach the 9th grade class and that 12th grade "regular" English, (which is really the "black English" in our school), was a good fit for me. Truth be told, I had never taught 12th grade English, and I had no desire to teach that class. I was upset but I told her that I would roll with the punches. After the horrible news, I asked the 12th grade, white, veteran teacher across the hallway for help. She had helped me with 10th grade English materials when I first arrived, but this time she said, "You're on your own...You've got it...You're a smart guy...You can handle it." She looked at me with cold eyes, eyes that spoke like a sign that read: "Niggers not welcome". There were plenty of times I questioned whether or not I was being treated differently because of my race. However, in this case the volume was turned up high and it blasted in my ear, the lack of concern causing my eardrums to throb.

I stand firmly with the knowledge that my treatment this year (along with the past five years) as a coach in Virginia would have been better if I was not a young black coach. Anyone who thinks differently should evaluate my case and write a book. Due to the nature of my year and the bleak future of my job in Fairfax County, I chose to quit and now I have begun to lay out the plans to open my *own* school in Maryland: The Maryland School of Excellence. Google it.

Chapter 6. The Law and its Application

In this day and time, one would expect the application of the law to individuals most certainly to be applied equally. We expect that if someone commits a crime in the school system, they would be turned in and prosecuted regardless of their race, religion, or ethnic background. After all, one would think that we have progressed as a society and have come to understand that a crime unpunished is a crime against civil obedience leading to certain civil disobedience. Still there are those in authority in the school system that knowingly allow some criminals to walk, not turning them in, while those of color are tracked down and turned in. This is not a statement for or the advocating of allowing those of color to walk, but instead a statement to bring about the fair implementation of the pursuit of criminals regardless of color. At the moment, that is not the case as will be illustrated in the following accounts of a criminal of color who was pursued and punished while a white criminal was not even pursued.

These are the tales of those cases involving two very similar individuals in their personalities but different in their color. Gary Parker who is white and Thadeus Coles who is black, both came to the school system supposedly with a desire to be mentors to and role models for those young men with whom they would come in contact. Both expressed their desire to do whatever was necessary to help build the confidence and self-esteem of the young men they would encounter. They had decided to try to do what they could to help the world become a better place by helping the young men become admirable men.

They both came to the school system by way of becoming assistant coaches for the football team. They had the desire to come in as teachers but lacked the credentials to do so, as neither had completed the necessary academic criteria for that position. Getting themselves involved with the athletic programs was their way in because the school system is always in need of coaching help. They both came into the system with the idea that they would eventually gain the teaching credentials by going back to school as they worked within the school system. This is something that many before them had done. Still, it takes a certain dedication in order to focus and put forth the effort that is necessary to produce the desired results.

Sadly theirs is a story that became sort of ironic. Their intent was to instill a desire to be successful in something and to convey the focus it takes to make it happen. That was their intent but the irony was that they could not do it for themselves. They failed to remained focused themselves in terms of acquiring the education they needed to become full-time teachers. As with many people when dreams aren't being realized self-doubt can begin to invade the private thoughts and rational thinking can become clouded. When someone has goals and they are not realized that opens up the opportunity for other vices to take hold and obstruct that person from pursuing their goals.

This was the case for both Gary and Thadeus. Gary had begun to have a hard time of keeping up with his bills and as a result he had to move out of his apartment. Being an assistant coach and substitute teaching did not quite provide the financial support that he needed to be independent. With nowhere to live and no family to fall back on, he wondered where he would go. He decided to turn to the principal for guidance in hopes that she would be able to give him some direction. As he explained his situation to the principal, she felt compassion for him and he was invited to take up residence with her and her husband until he could get his finances back in order.

Initially, things were going great for Gary as he had a place to live, a ride to work, and food to eat when he was hungry. This situation afforded Gary the opportunity to really get his finances in order to be able to pursue his credentials for teaching. He would no longer have to worry about his bills or how he would get to work. Some would say this was a golden opportunity. Gary spent a lot of time helping out as an assistant football coach and other after school activities. He was becoming a positive influence on those students and student-athletes he came into contact with.

However, when a golden opportunity comes along, how much gold is in that opportunity depends upon the person or persons for whom that opportunity presents itself. For Gary time began to catch up with him and with time comes the test of patience and dedication. When an individual is not patient, time may pressure some into taking measures to try to make things happen for them when they have not done things to be deserving of that reward. That same pressure may help others to understand the importance of perseverance and dedication. Those who choose to react when they are not prepared to do so will usually fall victim to mistakes that can be costly. For those who are able to persevere their patience is rewarded as their goals are usually realized.

As stated how golden a golden opportunity is depends upon the person to whom the opportunity is given. It turned out that for Gary that there was not very much gold in that opportunity. Time proved that he lacked the patience and dedication that would be necessary for him to persevere. He was not content with free living and free rides he wanted to have more in his pocket faster. He had been given the responsibility of helping with an athletic fundraiser and at the same time the opportunity to show that he was trustworthy. He was unable to control his compulsion and found himself using the fundraising money as if it was his own. That was his miscue and as a result it would take him back down the road he was previously able to avoid.

As a result of his miscue, he was unable to produce the money that was due to the school at the end of the fundraiser. This prompted the principal who had opened up her house to Gary, given him meals and rides, to have to make a decision. It was a decision that should have been obvious for someone in her position. When someone does something wrong the principal is in a position that, one would think, mandates him to take the necessary steps to have the offender prosecuted.

Yet she did not take those steps, the steps necessary to have Gary prosecuted. Instead she gave Gary a lecture as if he were a student and sent him on his way. His was not a severe punishment but he was now without a place to live and for the time being no source of income as he could no longer be a part of the school system that he had come to rely on. Still, his punishment was not as harsh as it could have been had the principal chose to pursue criminal charges against him. He had escaped having to face the students he had disappointed or the possible criminal consequences of his actions. He was free to go to begin again the journey to try to get his life together.

That was Gary's story and considering the circumstances, it only left him with a bruised ego but still the opportunity to move on. Now, the events that took place for Thadeus, although also criminal in nature, brought about different results. Just like Gary, Thadeus was an assistant coach for the football team at West Summit. He was also having a positive influence in many of the students that he came into contact with. He seemed to be ambitious and displayed an intellect, at times, that suggested that he belonged in a corporate setting that would promote his intuitiveness. He didn't seem to be someone who would embrace the prospect of grading papers and administering test. He was heavy into research, and given a topic, he could present it as if he had been involved with the subject all of his life.

Thomas Jones

Considering the way in which he presented himself, one had to wonder what had brought Thadeus to the school system, accepting a low paying entry level position. While speaking with him, the thought would have to cross one's mind as to why he would accept such a position. He was eager to expound upon subjects, but not so eager to expound upon his background. He would answer any question asked of him, even personal, but the personal answers were as vague as some of the intellectual answers he would give. The whole story as to why Thadeus had foregone the possibility of success in another area of society that would utilize his intellect for profit would never become known. It would seem that he might not be content with his status in life at the time.

What was known was that Thadeus still lived at home with his mother at the age of 38 and had no transportation of his own. As to whether he even had a driver license to operate a vehicle is still not known. It was well known that he relied on public transportation to get around. Still, Thadeus was now in a position that could give him the opportunity to enlighten the lives of some young people and possibly put himself in a position that would allow him to become independent. He could now take the necessary classes to obtain his teaching credentials while the school system would help him with the financial burden.

He became a very well-liked member of the staff at West Summit by both the students and the school staff. He was always willing to help when someone needed help no matter the time or day. All that was needed was to just to let him know the need and if there was something that he could do he was willing to do it.

Here was another person with a golden opportunity, but as mentioned how much gold is in an opportunity depends upon the person who has the opportunity. Thadeus seemed to have the dedication as he was promoting products for a company and had been doing so for the past ten years. The problem is that normally after promoting products for a considerable period of time, the person promoting that product usually becomes financially secure or moves on to something else because they have not become financially secure. This was not the case for Thadeus and he maintained his commitment to that company even though he had not become financially secure. His commitment might be in question because it seems that he was in a continual search for something that would turn him into that elusive title of "millionaire".

This left Thadeus open to the vices that will sometimes turn people into petty or even ferocious criminals. Fortunately he did not become ferocious. However, he did get involved in something that would bring law enforcement officials down upon him. Thadeus somehow happened upon a master key to the school, allowing him access to the school and to any room in the schools building. As to how he happened upon this master key will probably remain a mystery because he has given two versions of how it came into his possession. One is that a former employee of the school gave it to him when he left the school for other opportunities. The other is that he found the key one school afternoon as he was leaving the building to go home. The first seems plausible but is probably unlikely, as normally the keys that the employees are accounted for and have to be turned in by the employee before they are officially released from the schools system. In other words those keys are accounted for unless stolen. During the course of the school year, some computers came up missing from the school. With that key, supposedly, Thadeus took the opportunity to take leave of a few of the schools computers. I say supposedly, because it was never proven that he was the one who actually took the computers. Thadeus's problems came when the principal just happened to notice him coming into the building through a door that was locked. It was a door that required a master key to be unlocked. He checked to find out the time what time and dates that the stolen computers had taken place. It turned out that by coincidence the thefts took place during the times that Thadeus was located in the building after school hours. It turned out that he was. Since he was in the vicinity of the building in the capacity of an assistant coach, it gave him ample opportunity to steal away and remove some of the computers. The principal then checked to find out if Thadeus had been issued a master key to the school. He had not. With that information she called the head of school security into her office and gave the order to watch Thadeus find out for certain whether or not he had a master key. She didn't think that Thadeus would admit to having the key and with no solid evidence, she did not want him to know that she suspected anything. In a few short weeks, the head of security was able to observe

Thadeus using the master key to gain entrance into the building. He relayed that information to the principal and they both now believed that Thadeus was probably the one who had stolen the schools' computers.

Once the principal knew that Thadeus was using a master key, she called him into her office and questioned him about it. Thadeus denied having a key even with the principal telling him that the head of security had observed him using it to gain entrance into the building. His denial left the principal with a dilemma. Should she now contact the school systems administration and suggest that Thadeus might be the person responsible for the disappearance of the schools computers and let them handle it in their way or should she take Thadeus's word and let it go. She excused him from her office and began contemplating the decision. Not long after Thadeus had left her office, her decision was made. The decision was quick, with very little deliberation on her part. She decided to phone the school system's administrative offices. Not more than one week after that call, Thadeus was arrested and charged with illegal entry into the school and theft of the computers.

That was it! Gary, a white male goes free. Thadeus, a black male gets arrested. Both involved in criminal activity, but only the black male is arrested. Another case of a white person being in charge and having the authority to choose goes to jail and who goes free. We may live in different times, but let us not forget that times have not changed.

෧ೲ

Chapter 7. The Latino Experience

America has seen a rapid increase in the number of Latin immigrants who have chosen to migrate to this so called "land of the free and home of the brave." As they have come, they have found that freedom is subjective and bravery is found in their pursuit of freedom without oppression. They have displayed a tenacity to work hard, to remain humble, and a mindset to diligently pursue the American dream. They have now begun to face what white America does when it seems that others may achieve the same status that they enjoy in this "great country."

One Latin immigrant who has faced the subterfuges that take place when those white Americans who are in authority misuse their authority to keep people in their place is Mrs. Marta Young. Mrs. Young came to America when she was but a blossoming young 18 year-old Mexican immigrant. She came here with her mother who was able to enter the country on a working visa and found life to be much more pleasant than what she had left behind in Mexico. Her mother, working as a housekeeper for a Washington diplomat, found opportunities for her family may be more abundant here than in her country. She came to this country in hopes of ensuring a better life for her young daughter. Her hope was to get young Marta in college to pursue a not yet determined career. In her mind, just to be in college would be a step forward, determining what career to choose would come soon enough. Alas, that career choice would not come to fruition.

While living in Alexandria, Virginia, with her mother, young Marta met a young man who was just graduating from the local university with a Master's degree in Engineering, John Young. It was love at first sight for him and Marta grew to care for him. After dating for only six months, John proposed to her. Against the advice of John's parents but to the delight of Marta's mother at the young age of 20, Marta and John got married. John was the son of a wealthy real estate developer and had enjoyed the benefits of the connections his father had made as a real estate developer. Upon graduating from college, he was immediately given a job at the states department of transportation as a lead engineer. Five years after marriage, Marta gave birth to their first son and two years later she gave birth to another son. With a devoted wife, two sons, and a promising career, one would think that John would have been content with how his life was going. That was not the case as John began experimenting with drugs as his sons were coming of school age.

As a result, Marta spent the following 12 years trying to hang on to a stable family life as well as trying to help John battle his addiction. It was not to be, her lifestyle just as so many others who indulge in drugs slowly succumbed to his addiction and the drugs won.

In order to keep her sanity, they began to live separate lives as she would lock her door in order to have a peaceful night of sleep. While John was relegated to the guest bedroom, and thus their sleeping arrangement had been made. As their oldest son graduated from high school, they lost their house as a result of John not paying the bills because he was using most of his money to support his drug habit.

When they lost the house, Marta moved, with her other son who was still a year away from graduating high school, into a rented townhouse. Their oldest son, not wanting or unable to deal with the situation, moved to New York. Marta was left with the task of having to now get a job to support herself and her son. This was difficult as she had not completed college and had not held a job for the past 18 years. Fortunately, she was able to get a job within the school system as a teacher's assistant. The pay was meager but with the help of alimony, when she received from her husbands garnished wages she was able to get by.

Not having John around in a white world is when her awakening to the pride and prejudice that she had been sheltered from for so long took place. Being married to a white man, she was unaware or of or unconscious of the prejudice surrounding her. She was previously granted the respect of her husband, but now when she ventured out, she was venturing out as just another immigrant. Now, being on her own, away from the protection of her husband, Marta had to deal with the reality of life in America as a person who is not white. She would come to find out that the white people in the school system would not treat any differently than those white people in the streets.

Because of a sudden need, Marta was placed in the main office of the school as an administrative assistant. With an opportunity to move up, she thought, within the school system, from a teachers' assistant to an administrative assistant, she could make more money. That opportunity was squelched. Mrs. Wallace, the principal of the school who was white, had other ideas for the position. After working for two years still getting the same pay as a teachers' assistant, Marta thought the only way she was going to get the pay that she knew she deserved was to ask for it. She did and was told that it would have to be discussed at the beginning of the following school year. When that year came Marta was surprised at what she came back to. In her place was a white woman and Marta had been moved to a position to run the schools detention program, which paid the same as her teachers assistant position. She would later find out that the woman who was now in her place was a friend of Mrs. Wallace. Marta decided to approach Mrs. Wallace to find out why she had been placed in a different position.

After two weeks of persistence, she was finally able to have the opportunity to talk with Mrs. Wallace. Previously Mrs. Wallace would always have things that were coming up and would profess that she really wanted to talk with Marta but her schedule was getting in the way. Marta felt that she was being avoided because

Mrs. Wallace had unfairly moved her and placed her friend in Marta's position. When she finally sat down with Mrs. Wallace she asked her why she was moved and not given the opportunity to remain in the position. Mrs. Wallace told her that she needed her in the position that she had placed her in and besides the other position pays less money. It was true that she did indeed need someone to fill the position that she placed Marta in, but it was not true about the pay. Marta accepted her explanation because she did not want to cause any problems. She later found out that the administrative assistants pay was $17,000 more than hers. Still she did not contest the decision of Mrs. Wallace because she feared that if she did she would be fired. Eventually Marta gained the courage to take a stand against Mrs. Wallace.

She found the courage when Mrs. Wallace was pressuring her to do something that she knew was wrong and she did not want to completely jeopardize her position in the school system. Mrs. Wallace was adamant about having Marta change numbers on a detention detail form that Marta had submitted to reflect the number that she wanted. Marta reluctantly did so, but made sure that she had stated on the form that it was at the request of Mrs. Wallace that the numbers were changed. Mrs. Wallace soon grew tired of Marta not jumping at her very whim and, when the opportunity presented itself, she had Marta removed from the school. Feeling completely betrayed Marta felt that she had to do something. Expressing her desire to do something about the situation she was told by other staff members that Mrs. Wallace had a lot of power in the County and it would be best if she just left things as they are. Marta went through all the channels that were available to her try to maintain her position but was refuted. An investigation took place but to no avail. Suffice it to say that, even with Mrs. Wallace admitting that she had done things that were inappropriate and the person doing the investigation having found that Mrs. Wallace had indeed had Marta commit fraud by changing numbers, Marta could get no justice.

When Marta had first detailed all that had happened he had assured her that if in fact these things had taken place Mrs. Wallace must be removed from her position. Of, course it is open for speculation but surely someone had made him change his mind. His response now was that Marta should have come to them immediately and because she had not there was nothing they could do. One would think that fraud is fraud regardless of when it is reported. The fact is the act took place within the school year. Surprisingly, Marta was told that she had no case and was encouraged to "leave it alone". Marta has tried to reach the schools superintendent but to no avail as she gets shuffled from one person to another, another indication that she is only considered a peon in the system. Mrs. Wallace continues to conduct herself in the way she sees fit. Another example of the "good ol' boy" network at work, only this time it was a white woman misusing the power instead of a white man.

∾∾

Chapter 8. The Political Effect

The political ramification of racism in schools is definitely something that has not been studied; possibly discussed but not studied. Although I am "enlightening" some of you who would not think that these things go on in schools, and I do not claim to be an expert on the subject. I am merely giving my individual view of some situations. In doing so, I would like to point out and comment on three particular incidents that shed further light on the fact that many whites have come to the understanding that they can and will get away with what they want to in the school system. It is political in the sense that white people are able to contact individuals within the school system who are able to keep them from facing consequences for their actions when they have done something wrong.

The following story is one given to me by Ms. Linda Stevenson who had the privilege of working as an instructional assistant in Allegany County, Maryland.

I came to Allegany County in the summer of 1962. I had met and married a man who was born and raised in Allegany County. Between the years of 1962 and 1965, my husband and I searched the Cumberland area wanting to rent, buy or build a home in a nice locale of the city. Back then we were referred to as "colored people". I can remember calling about properties on Hilltop Drive, Louisiana Avenue, White Oaks Development and the outer streets on and off Frederick Street.

In each and every case I would actually be asked, "Are you colored?", then we would be told, "We don't rent or sell to colored people. Colored people can't live in this neighborhood, don't live in this neighborhood, and aren't wanted in this neighborhood." At the time colored people mainly lived on Columbia Street, Independence Street, Central Avenue, Pine Avenue, Glen Wood Street or in the projects - Fort Cumberland Homes, Jane Frazier Village, or Benjamin Banneker. Now, as a parent, where would you want to raise your children?

The hope would be that such a culture in the county would have changed since that time. Sadly, that is not the case and the following story depicts the state of the county as I write this narrative.

A young black mother seeking to move her two daughters from the dangerous streets of her Washington, DC neighborhood, decided to move to Cumberland, Maryland in hopes of raising her daughters in a more peaceful lifestyle. She had no idea what she was about to subject her and her daughters to. It has been said that ignorance is bliss, but the thought of racial ignorance is probably not thought of when that maxim is used. She had come to an area where there were only approximately 20 black students out of a population of approximately 1,000 students. Social isolation and racially motivated attacks are always looming with such a low number of minorities in a school. With new "meat" coming to the school, it opened up that possibility. The blacks who were in the school had grown up with the white students and those white students didn't see them as a threat to their way of life, but someone coming from the outside that could be a different story. Racial ignorance can be just as dangerous as the physical dangers she had sought to free her daughters of, but that had not entered her mind.

That is exactly what she and her daughters came up against—racial ignorance. As school began, her daughters became the unwitting targets of racial slurs on the way to the bus stop, on the school bus, and while in school. This type of ignorance was not something that their mother had expected. Still, it was taking place and she had to find a way to deal with it.

Just as most young people would want to do, the girls' had wanted to take matters into their own hands but their mother had taught them better and they didn't. They talked with their mother, seeking advice on how to handle the fire that was building inside of them. Initially she talked with her daughters about the ills of racism and the travails that her ancestors had gone through in order for them to be able to live a life without the degradation that they dealt with. She told them to stand strong, hold their heads up, and not to allow this ignorance to get them down and it would soon pass.

That was not the case and the insults continued to the point of bringing the girls to tears. Their mother thought that the best thing to do would be to go to the principal for some empathy and support to bring the troubles to an end. He assured her that those types of acts would not be tolerated and he would put a plan in place to alleviate the situation. He took the names of the students of whom the girls knew were causing them problems and the mother and her daughters went home, believing that something positive would take place. She had taught her daughters that seeking justice through authority is always the best approach to solving problems. So she did that and was hoping that something would change.

That hope was dashed as her daughters came back to her with the same dire and disgusted look as they had before. The racial remarks had not stopped and they were now at their wits end, finding it very difficult not to retaliate. Their mother continued to keep them calm as she again approached the principal about the situation. It seems he did not have the time to address the problem with the other students himself and had delegated that task to an assistant. She came to find out that the assistant, who lives in the same neighborhood as those students, only had a casual conversation with the students in question. He simply asked them to cease their taunts, but no direct demand was made of them. As most school personnel know, if there is no direct demand of a student, there will likely be no direct action on the students' part to adhere to what is being asked. After finding this out she decided to visit the principal again. When she approached the principal about this, he again assured her that he would have the problem taken care of, this time personally. Of course, wanting to believe the integrity of the statement, she took his word for it and went home.

Again, that hoped was soon dashed as the girl's came home once again practically in tears because of the taunts. Their mother decided that she needed to go above the principal and decided to go to the school board in hope of finally receiving some sort of justice. She did just that, thinking that surely this would bring about some change. Still, it did not and she was beginning to feel helpless and hopeless because she felt that she was running out of options of who to turn to for help. She had tried to handle it herself and it did not work, she had gone to the principal with no results, and she had gone to the school board and no relief. She began to think that the best thing to do is to just give up and allow racism to win and move back to Washington, DC. Surely mental peace of mind is just as important as physical safety. At least with the physical aspect there is an understanding that it will probably not be an everyday occurrence.

As she contemplated the move back to Washington, DC she had a conversation with a friend who convinced her to first try talking with the NAACP. That friend reminded her that if she allowed them to run her out, they will continue with the state of mind that they can control the lives of black people and the next black family who decides to try for a more peaceful way of life will run into the same thing. But if she could just fight it, it might bring about some change and make a way for other families to be able to enjoy that peaceful way of life. She decided to take that friend's advice and contacted the NAACP.

After listening to the mother's description of the situation, the NAACP decided to take up the cause with her in hopes of bringing about some change. The need to involve the NAACP sheds light on how deeply rooted hatred can be. As word spread, and the media got word out that the NAACP was to visit the school, those who are racist came out in droves. Many of the students began to wear, more than before, their confederate hats, bandanas, shirts, and jackets. Parents had pulled in front of the school, on the day the NAACP was to arrive, with their confederate flags hanging on their trucks, or just standing holding it in their hands. Of course the typical argument always follows that the flag does not represent racism, it represents heritage. The truth of the matter is that such heritage is one of oppression and racism. Further, the flag signifies the desire to maintain the oppression and racism. That is why anytime there is something dealing with racial injustice, that flag continues to come out and NEVER comes out when it comes to dealing with racial unity.

After the NAACP became involved, the school's board of education agreed to put into place benchmarks to achieve to help erode the racial prejudice that was permeating their county. To this day, that plan has to yet to come to fruition and clearly there will not be any benchmarks met. As the girls left the county, the news media stepped back, the county went back to business as usual and nothing has moved forward in terms of racial socialization. It seems that the county did what it thought necessary to alleviate the bad publicity that they were receiving and once it was alleviated they saw no reason to go any further.

The problem with that line of thinking is that eventually a time might come where racial tension could escalate without warning. In fact it did. As a predominantly black football team from Washington DC made its way to play one of the county's elite and nationally known football team, they could not predict the racial situation upon which they were embarking.

The team took the field and racial slurs were immediately directed their way. The players initially tried to ignore them but it became so constant that they could not take it anymore. The taunts were not only coming from the spectators but also from the opposing players on the field. The coach approached a game official about the situation, but he denied hearing anything and refused to address the issue. The least he could have done was to relay the coach's concerns to the opposing coach, but he chose to ignore it. As a result, even though they were winning the game at the time, the coach decided it would be best if he removed his team from field. If he had he allowed his team to remain on the field, the consequences might have been far worst than just a loss as a result of forfeiture. The result could have been emotional scarring of young minds, emotions running to the point of retaliation and fighting and of course the result would have undoubtedly been a riot. In the event of a riot, there is no doubt the stigma that would have been placed on the Washington players as a result. The coach did the right thing. Still, the school, its players and coaches and county spokespeople deny any racial slurs took place. History has shown that denial is always the stance that those who commit such acts take, and later the proof comes out. The county is in real need of racial awareness.

Back at West Summit, young Tiffany James, a black female student was in a History class with a white male teacher, Mr. Brand, who had been teaching for 30 years. Mr. Brand, of course, felt that he was untouchable as long as he didn't molest any students. After concluding a discussion with his class on the history of slavery, he made a comment to Tiffany that is almost unforgivable. He told her—"If I were a slave master I would have you as my slave to do my bidding". She, being young, did not know how to respond and simply said nothing. When she made me aware of what had happened, I immediately went to the principal and let him know what had happened. He said that he would speak with Mr. Brand about what had happened. After about two weeks, he finally got back to me and said that Mr. Brand acknowledgement that it was bad judgment on his part to make such a statement. After several emails back and forth between me and the principal as to what reprimand would be given to Mr. Brand, I was told that Mr. Brand had 30 years of experience in teaching and one mistake should not warrant a reprimand. In subsequent emails, I outlined the various other instances that Mr. Brand had used racially insensitive language toward minorities. One instance was his yelling at one of the black track athletes to "run like the police was chasing you". I informed him that many of the black faculty had expressed their concerns about the way in which Mr. Brand speaks to black students when no one is around. Still, the principal made excuses for Mr. Brand's actions. After all the discussions, I have not approached the subject with the principal again. However, I did let him know that many of the silent black faculty members feared repercussions for speaking up because they feel that Mr. Brand is untouchable. Sadly, it appears that he is untouchable as he remains in the school system and continues to make racially insensitive remarks. Sometimes he is even bold enough to make those remarks in front of other staff members.

As young black students witness that any white teacher is allowed to denigrate them with no consequences, it has to have a psychological effect on them. Contextually, over the past 15 years, African American males' perception of the world may be contingent upon their upbringing, background, and their style of communication, which may ultimately affect how they process information in school (Durody&Hirdeth,1995). Eventually, these contextual factors may have an adverse affect on their academic performance in school and could become predictors of success (Berends&Koertz, 1995, 1996). The question becomes how concerned is the system with the overall perception of how these students view themselves and their success in school.

Political pundits, radio and TV talk show hosts, continue to boast about the racial acceptance of America. They contend that racism does not play a role in the success of blacks in America. They don't believe that there is still a need for affirmative action in America.

They try to promote the idea that blacks have just as much of a chance of getting a job as a white person. They simply ignore the fact that after 40 years of civil rights, only 30 of those years have brought about equal rights, and only about 20 of those years have brought about semblance of equal opportunity. They want to believe that those few years have erased over 200 years of bondage both mentally and physically. It takes generations to train a race to accept, trust, and interact in a productive manner after being in bondage for so many years. They ignore the fact, that given the opportunity to choose between a young black man or a young white man with the same credentials, those prominent white people who are in power will choose the young white man. Just as the football coach asserted that he has connections and could ruin a kid, those prominent white people who have even more connections, could make or break an individual if they so choose.

As has been noted, there are enough white people in prominent positions that could allow for the progression and success of blacks in America. Those same prominent people could be influential in assuring that success is denied in the corporate world. It is easy for one to say how someone should be able to come out of a depressed situation but the reality is that it is a more difficult task than they could truly imagine if they have not been in it.

What would their state in life be if their ancestors had instilled in them the fact that, even after being freed they could trust no man? What if they found themselves in the midst of a country of plenty yet they were hungry? What if they had the ability to work but no one was willing to allow them to work to improve their state in life. Without having that understanding, they cannot truly appreciate the hardships that black America has had to endure. Those pundits can choose to deny that corporate America is run by white America if they so choose. I say if they do deny this fact, they may as well deny other obvious truths such as that they are themselves white.

With all that I have said, it will be a great surprise to many that I am no great proponent of affirmative action. You may wonder how I could make such a statement. It is because I do recognize that there are enough prominent black people in America to have a positive affect on the state of black America. However, the truth of the matter is they seem to have no more of a desire to do so than do prominent white people. Those political pundits believe that because of this, blacks should be able to make their own way. In time, maybe that will come to be. But until then, something needs to be in place to assure that there are equal opportunities.

The country needs to come to terms with the fact that we have only been free for 100 years and to think that 200 years of institutionalized slavery can be vanquished from the minds of a people is preposterous. They have been in charge for the past 300 years in America and still don't have it right in a system they created. Give us time and we will find a way to make it work. Give us the resources that whites have had for these 300 years, the disposable income to cover up our mistakes and just see how far we can progress in 300 years.

❧❧

Chapter 9. The reality of it all

This narrative is not meant to be an indictment of all of the white teachers and administrators of the public school system of America, but it is meant to bring to light the fact that we are still oppressed and consistently labor under the threat of oppression. This narrative is meant to, hopefully, make some of those in power take a step back and look at how they might have allowed oppression to take place and decide to not allow it to continue. It is meant to encourage those who have sat back and allowed those in power to oppress them to take a stance when it is happening to them and take the necessary steps to alleviate it.

Racism, prejudice, and the social ladder landscape are in place in America. As the black teacher goes into the classroom, these are obstacles that they are trying to teach the children to overcome while also teaching them the school's curriculum. They understand what the students have to deal with everyday and how the social world impacts not only their ability to learn but also how they learn and why some of them strive to beat the system. Their parents' values, morals, attitudes, and social relationships continuously influence the students' character and quite often those tenets differ from what their teachers are trying to convey.

Teachers are also in a constant battle against those in the entertainment business who continue to promote negative values. I speak directly toward the world of sports and music. In radio, what the host of many of the shows may say will be contradicted by the music they play. For example one talk show host talked about the need to promote positive self-esteem within our black communities. After making that statement, the next song they played had lyrics that promoted the idea of looking for a mate that would be from the hood (an attitude of don't let anyone tell you what to do, it's about survival). The lyrics listed the qualities of someone being from the hood as "always being ready to fight", "Thugged out. From the hood.", "I like my thugs from every city." "The ones that talk so hood." "Down for whatever." Those who play those songs on the radio may certainly debate the innocence of those lyrics, but we know the reality of those lyrics mean. Most of those who are experiencing success in those two areas are very young and immature. As a result their view of the world and how one should migrate in the world is seen through an immature mind. That statement is not meant as an insult as we are all immature when we are young. I would be the first to say that we mature over years. These young artists are reacting and speaking from what they have experienced in the world and for most of them they believe they have experienced enough to know how the world moves. It takes years of living in the world to come to the understanding that they don't know as much as they thought they knew and nothing can give them those years of experience in the world until they have actually lived through those years.

Although some of them continue to cling to immature ideas when they get older, most come to understand that many of those negative values will have a negative impact on them and their children. When they come to that understanding, they begin to map out a different plan for their children. The things that they may have done at a young age they now restrict their children from doing because they now "know" the negative consequences of it.

Those who are in power who can change that landscape either have no desire to do so, are afraid to do so because they fear being "cut off" from their aspirations by those who are more powerful and do not want to change. Or more sadly, they lack the knowledge to do so. They have come to be in the position they are in, not because of their intellect, but because of who they knew. Even more depressing is the fact that some of those who have the power to bring about that change are not only those who are white but many who are black.

Black people, on a whole, have sat back and watched those who rise in power as a result of their coming on the scene when something transcending may be happening. Once on the scene, they make a name for themselves or keep their name in the public spotlight and capitalize on it. I could name those whose pockets have benefited, but I am sure it is not necessary as they and most who read this are fully aware of who they are. They are the ones that whenever something goes wrong, they are the first to look for the cameras and newspapers to offer a statement. As a people, we have allowed these self-appointed spokesmen to continue to go from scene to scene and profit from it. We have not demanded that they stop going from scene to scene and begin to initiate their own scenes. They are in a position to bring about real change, but their focus is always on the immediate situation taking place rather than taking time to really sit down and put a plan in place that can bring about some real changes.

It is time for black people as a whole, when they see those people coming to tell them we don't need them coming now that the spotlight is on. Justice will be served as a result of the spotlight and their sharing in the spotlight will not make a difference. When we do that, maybe they will wake up and realize that they can no longer be scavengers benefiting from the troubles of others but it is time for them to use their status to truly uplift their race. Sure, they have founded some non-profit organizations that have provided opportunities for a few, but those organizations really only serve as a tax shelter that lines their pockets. It would only take a little bit of time and effort for them to put together for-profit business projects that could benefit a greater number of people. However, this doesn't take place because it doesn't offer a large profit for their pockets and it would also require real work on their part. Not only that, they have the fear of a failed business attached to their name resulting in, what they probably believe, an unfavorable public scrutiny possibly damaging their reputation.

I am going to say some things about our president (Obama) that may not be agreeable to many, but I feel that I must say them. What a wonderful thing it is that has happened, a black man has become president of the United States of America. First of all, is he really the first? That is a question that many blacks would really rather not fathom, but it is nonetheless a question that should be addressed. Not wanting to know the truth is one of things that blacks, as well as Americans in general, continues to hold onto. That problem has helped America to remain in the state of confusion about race. For instance, did Abraham Lincoln have any black blood in him, what about Warren G Harding, his lineage has yet to be truly addressed. As we know, many blacks "passed" for white during Warren G. Harding's time and the truth about how and why he died may never be told.

Secondly, although Obama's skin tone is that of a black man, he has not really lived the life style of a black man. Again, let's get real, his mother was white and his father left at an early age. He grew up with his white mother in a white family setting and spent a lot of time with his white grandmother and their family setting. Theirs were not the everyday surroundings of the lifestyle that black people live. His was not hearing about the struggles that black people have to deal with in terms of racism and prejudices that everyday black people deal with. His was not the everyday understanding that mommy or daddy did not get a promotion or job because he or she was black. His was not the everyday understanding of how black people interact with each other as a family, a neighborhood, at parties, in controversy and camaraderie. He did not get the true dynamic of a black persons' lifestyle and just as a white man can never truly understand it neither can he. This dynamic is something that you have to live in order to truly understand it and nothing can be said or done to help someone to truly understand it if they have not lived it.

Finally, although it has often been asked, what has he really done? His opponents ask in terms of his being a part of political accomplishments and their only goal is to win a political race (no pun intended). I ask in terms of his bringing to light the plight of the black man and my goal is to bring to light the importance of our finding some true leaders who make the scene instead of coming on to the scene. Great, he is in office, but what did he do along the way? He lead no movement that brought about any great change for the black man. He helped no significantly large group of black people begin businesses that could potentially put thousands of black people to work. He turned no ghetto into a thriving community, and he didn't "reach back" or "pull up" anybody who has spent their whole life trying to "get up". He talked the talk with those who could help him, walked the walk with those who could elevate him, and he distanced himself from those who could not promote him. Don't get me wrong, I don't agree with many of the views of some of those he distanced himself from, but let's get real, and stop dodging the truth. You don't just come to know someone all of a sudden, if you have known them for over 20 years and then decide you no longer want to be associated with them. Their views didn't change overnight because they were exposed by the media. You knew who they were before then, but they had a positive impact on what you were doing at the time so you clung to them.

I leave you with this thought as was once quoted as a caption below a picture on a t-shirt produced by a budding young black artist fresh out of college by the name of Billy Colbert—"Malcolm and Martin are gone, now is the time for us to put our heads together and come up with some real solutions." If we don't, we condemn ourselves by accepting the fate that our so-called leaders have mapped out for us.

Indeed it is a bright future for them, but a lifelong struggle for the masses of black people holding on to their hope for a change that will not come. We have accepted the idea that an African American being elected as the "first" African American President as a victory in this "racial war". I say we have completely lost sight of what the goal should be and that is to win the war of bringing our people the opportunity to avail themselves of all that America has to offer. We have to realize that the power doesn't rest in the political offices won but in deeply establishing ourselves in the corporate structure that runs America. We have the people, the resources, and the financial power, but we have not put the infrastructure into place to contend. We could benefit by taking a page from Jewish Americans. They have not been concerned with political power but they have put into place an infrastructure that has allowed ALL of their people to thrive and we can do the same.

REFERENCES

Berends, M., & Koretz, D. (1995-1996. Reporting minority students' test scores: How well can the national assessment of educational progress account for differences in social context [Electronic version]. Educational Assessment, 3(3), 249-285.

Durodoy, B., & Hidreth, B. (1995). Learning styles of the African American student [Electronic version]. Journal of Negro Studies.